D1011154

the
wOman'S
bOoK

of

Simple
Delights

The Woman's Book of

Simple Delights

More than 200
Everyday Indulgences

by Kerry Colburn
Illustrated by Debbie Hanley

RUNNING PRESS
PHILADELPHIA · LONDON

A Running Press® Miniature Edition™
© 2003 by Running Press
All rights reserved under the Pan-American
and International Copyright Conventions

Printed in China

Library of Congress Cataloging-in-Publication Number 2002108260

ISBN: 978-0-7624-1485-7

This book may be ordered by mail from the publisher.
Please include $1.00 for postage and handling.
But try your bookstore first!

Running Press Book Publishers
2300 Chestnut Street
Philadelphia, PA 19103-4371

Visit us on the web!
www.runningpress.com

GET READY
for
serious
pampering!

I t's no secret that we women ought to take better care of ourselves—and that doesn't just mean another trip to the gym, a better night's sleep, or more leafy green vegetables. Gosh, no!

There are times when our regular routine—no matter how healthy, balanced, or fun—just isn't enough. We need some pampering, some serious caretaking, and let's face it, sometimes there's no one who can do it like we can.

Remember, it's okay to be a little selfish or decadent when an overextended brain, body, or heart demands it! Maybe we've suffered through a bad breakup. Maybe there are problems at work. Maybe we're planning a wed-

ding, helping a friend through a cri-
sis, grieving a loss, recovering from a
family event, or just plain stretched
too thin. Whatever the reason, during
these periods there's a little voice inside
that reminds us that we should be tak-
ing extra-good care of ourselves. Can't
you hear it?

Unfortunately, the truth is that if
we are particularly busy, discouraged,
or emotionally drained, we are less
likely to listen. No more! When what's

happening in our lives becomes a whirlwind that leaves us skimping on ourselves, when we find ourselves saying, "I'll do something nice for myself next week" and that turns into next month, when we start feeling run down or worn out, it's high time for some well-earned pampering of the body, mind, and spirit. It's time to take it to the next level. It's time for Simple Delights!

The following are easy pick-meups that bring the focus back to you. Most can be fast, many are free, some involve friends, and others are solitary. Flip through the book and see which ones leap out at you, pique your interest, or make you smile, and choose what's most appealing for your current mood. Then, without having to invest too much time or effort, you can give in and give yourself a little lift. As any of your best girlfriends would agree, you deserve it!

Wear your
AbsOlute greAteSt
pair of shoes
(even if they're out *of* season)

OR

**Try on a dozen
new liPsticks until
you find a winner**

Make a list of
the best compliments you've
ever received

OR

Go through your old
photo albums and laugh
(and realize how
great you look now!)

Bake
sweet-smelling
gingerbread cookies
(and don't share them)

OR

Pet puppies at
the local animal shelter

Paint
your toenails a
coLor you've nevEr dreAmt
of wearing

OR

Read a
tRashy magaZine
in the tub with
the phOne tuRned off

[14]

Try on couture gowns
at a fancy boutique

OR

Take a hike with
binoculars and a notepad to
record your thoughts

Sing loudly to Aretha Franklin
in the shower

OR

Snap photos of picturesque
places in your town

Tape a soap opera
all week and then watch it
on Friday night (and
don't forget the popcorn!)

OR

Get out your old love
letters and remind yourself
how lovable you are
(and always have been!)

Dress up and
treat yourself to an
exquisite lunch at a fancy
restaurant (complete with
champagne cocktail)

OR

Dress up and try on
expensive jewelry at Tiffany's

Spend a
fuLL hAlf-hOur
at a great florist *or* greenhouse
(floral smells
are a natural high!)

OR

Buy a yummy
essential oil and diffuser
fOr your BedRoOm

[21]

Buy pRetty pOstcards
to put on your fridge

OR

Tear out inspirational
magaZine
*o*r
cAtalog phOtos
of what your
ideal home looks like

[22]

Spend an afternoon
at an art gallery

OR

Go to a small neighborhood
branch library and browse
all afternoon (don't you love
that old book smell?)

Skip rocks at
the beach or riverbank

OR

Get a one-day pass
at a local Y and
spend an hour swimming
and splashing

LiGht candLes and
liSten to MoZart
as you get ready for work
in the morning

OR

LiGHt CaNDLeS AND
listen to Mozart
in your office at the end
of a rough day

[27]

Try on a favorite outfit
and admire how great you look

OR

Pick up your childhood
favorite ice cream treat from a
neighborhood market

Reread a Jane Austen novel
all day while drinking tea

OR

Write bad poetry
on your front porch

Get all the ingredients
tO mAke yourSeLf
and a friend really elaborate
GiRL DRiNkS
(fresh banana daiquiris, B-52s,
frOzen cosmos...)

OR

Let yourself have
total stillness for 15 minutes
iN the miDdle Of the day

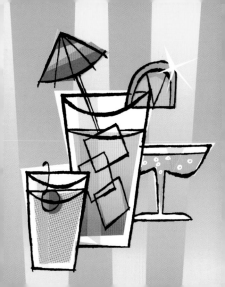

SOak your haiR
in a hot-oil treatment

OR

Go shopping
for one very specific
and nOn-practical thing
you've always wanted,
like kidSkin glOves
oR a rHineStone tiAra

Buy a lovely art book
you've never heard of and put it
on your coffee table

OR

Pick up brochures
about exotic places from
a travel agency and daydream

Visit a friend or neighbor's
new baby to cuddle and coo

OR

Sign up for an introductory
class in a craft you've
always been interested in—
knitting, photography,
basket weaving

Hit tennis
balls against a wall
at the park

OR

Shoot baskets

Send yourself flowers
for no reason

OR

Send your mother,
grandmother, or best friend
flowers for no reason

Brush your hair
oNe hundred tiMes with
a terrific hairbrush

OR

Pumice your feet,
coat with peppermint
lotion, and put on
tHick coTTon sOcks

Bring your favorite
childhood lunch to work,
including a thermos
oF miLk and a fuNny nOte
(trading with co-workers
is allowed)

OR

MAKE A POT OF
savory homemade soup

Pick up free samples
of expensive face masks at
a department store

OR

Fly a kite

Dance to Madonna in front
of a mirror

OR

Drive through your
favorite city park with cheesy
pop music on the stereo

RENT FiVE GREAT
girl movies,
make a bed on the
liVing rOoM flOor, and hAve
a weekend marathon

OR

Wander through a bookstore
that'S oPen in the
evening, buying one
"staff pick"

[45]

Go card shopping
and send surprise notes
to friends

OR

Take your coffee and
the newspaper back to bed
with you on Sunday

Watch Saturday morning
cartoons while eating
your favorite childhood cereal

OR

Go for a walk
in a neighborhood that
you never visit

Shine
your favorite
shoes

OR

Start a scrapbook
Of fAVORiTE MEMoRIES
of the year

Have a cold beer
in your yard late at night,
looking at the stars

OR

Attempt a cartwheel

Try on fabulous hats
with a friend

OR

Read a page-turning
bodice ripper at a coffee shop
all afternoon

Turn on flattering
lights and admire your body
in a full-length mirror

OR

Find a reputable
"adult" store, don dark glasses,
and start shopping

Buy the most recent
issue of three magazines
you never read
and sit on a park bench

OR

Put on a snazzy outfit,
call a snazzy friend, and
have a drink at the snazziest
hotel bar in town

See a matinee of
a fOreign fiLm yOu've
never heard of

OR

SiT OuTSiDE
and listen to the birds

Go tO A DRoP-IN YoGA
or meditation class

OR

Offer to walk
a friend's dog

Drive to the closest body
of water and put your feet in

OR

Lay down after work with
chamomile tea bags on
your eyes and your favorite
CD playing

Make yourself a
hot-fudge sundae with
all the trimmings
(don't forget the cherry)
to eat in bed

OR

Write down your dreams
in a bedside journal

Make s'mores

OR

Try skipping around
the block

Check out an unfamiliar
opera or jazz recording
from your library

OR

Feed the ducks

Kiss someone
you've always meant to

OR

PLaNT SoME TuLiPS

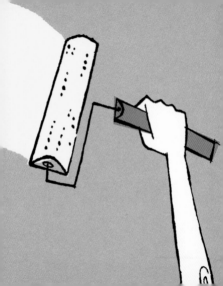

Rent
RoLLeR SKaTES

OR

PaINT YoUR
bathroom a warm,
fLattering cOlor

Take a drive to
a nearby town or
NEiGHBoRHOOD
you've always wanted to see

OR

GeT A FACIaL
at a beauty school

Get a gReat boOk-*o*N-tape
and drive aimlessly
all day on Sunday

OR

Make yourself
an ultimate brunch:
WAF*ſ*LES, WhIPPED CReAM,
strawberries, fresh juice,
cloth n*a*pkins

Wear your most comfortable
article of clothing
all day long, no matter
its condition

OR

Drink all your beverages
through a Crazy Straw

Read through
your old yearbook

OR

Go to an
outdoor concert

Invite a friend over
for jump rope and hopscotch
on the sidewalk

OR

Stroll barefoot through
an arboretum or public garden

Reread your favorite
childhood book

OR

Buy yourself
beautiful silk pajamas

Rent a canoe or kayak
and contemplate life

OR

Steam your face over
a bOiling pot oF water
infused with
DRiED LAVeNdER

[75]

Spend an afternoon at a flea market, unearthing one great find (even if it's a fixer-upper)

OR

Find a carnival advertised in the newspaper and ride the Ferris wheel

Test drive
sexy convertibles on
a sunny day

OR

Practice
your signature
with a fountain pen

Make a homemade
body scrub from salt, sesame
oil, and fresh lemon

OR

Rent a yoga video

Mat and frame
a treasured family photo

OR

Find a friend
who knits and start a
project together

Paint your nails
candy apple red

OR

Have a complimentary
makeover at a
cosmetics counter

Go for a professional
blow-out or up-do before
a night out

OR

Play Frisbee with
a friend

Go to an
observation point
oR sceNic overloOk
to get some perspective

OR

Visit a day spa
for one treatment
you've never tried before

Go shell-hunting
on a beach

OR

Test drive
false eyelashes

Wear your special-
occasion underwear even
though it's Monday

OR

Drink your
morning juice out of a
champagne flute

Drop in on a belly dancing
or tAi chi cLass

OR

Make homemade
SuSHi

[8 7]

Buy a bag of rose petals
from a florist and scatter them
around your house

OR

Buy a potted orchid
for your desk

Go to a
community
pancake breakfast

OR

Play pool and shoot darts
at a tavern when
you're technically supposed
to be at work

Pick up bubbles and pinwheels
at the five-and-dime

OR

Make one comfort recipe
from childhood

Get your car
washed at a school
fundraiser

OR

Have your tarot cards read

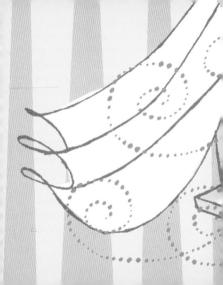

Sit on your porch
or in your open window,
BReAthiNg iN
fresh air

OR

**Go to
ThE SyMPHoNY**

Test perfumes
until you find your favorite

OR

Add ESSENTiAL OiL
tO A water spritZer and
spray your house
or office

Invest in sumptuous
400-thread-count sheets

OR

Burn a CD
of feel-good songs

Try a new wine
you've never heard of

OR

Make
chocolate fondue

Take a
train ride

OR

Put windchimes
iN YoUR BeDROoM WiNdoW

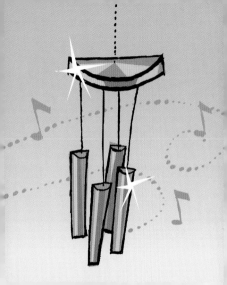

Go to an
AuthOr REading at
a bookstore

OR

Take a long
LuNch bReak
and catch *a* matinee

Subscribe to a magazine
that you secretly love

OR

Give your hands a soothing
paraffin treatment

Go to a bar
and order a kir royale

OR

Read Shakespeare sonnets
by candlelight

Go to a local
high school play

OR

Buy
last-minute
discount
OPeRA TiCKETS

Compose a personal ad
highlighting your best qualities

OR

Hit the tasting room
at a local winery

Plan a road trip to
see a friend

OR

Buy a small bouquet for
your nightstand

Hire a maid service
for the day

OR

Spend some quality time
iN A BAKeRY

Send a book
from your shelf
to a *friend*
you know will love it
(and remember to inscribe it)

OR

BufF YOUR NAiLs
to a high shine

Go to the free night at
a local museum

OR

Visit a sculpture garden

Book a solo night at a cozy,
quiet bed-and-breakfast

OR

Finally sign up for
that seminar
or lecture you've been
thinking about

Take a long walk

OR

REaRRANgE
the furniture in your bedroom
or living room

Go to a nearby
playground and play
on the swings

OR

Set up a hammock
and use it

Climb a tree

OR

Splash through puddles
in galoshes

Light every single candle
in your house

OR

COLLeCT LeAVES

String twinkly lights along your
fence or bedroom window

OR

Put on sparkly eye shadow

Have your palm read

OR

Visit a friend
who has a hot tub

Take a
salsa lesson

OR

Buy
fishNeT SToCKiNGS
and wear them to a meeting
you're dreading

Simmer hot cider
with cinnamon sticks on your
stove all afternoon

OR

Bring out holiday cards
from last year and remind yourself what great friends you have

Head to the zoo
on a sunny afternoon and
overcome your fear of snakes
and komodo dragons

OR

Visit a craft fair
or public art show

PUT oN
a floral dress
(AnD MAYBE EvEN
GLoVES)
and meet girlfriends
for high tea

OR

Throw your sheets or
towels in the dryer
right before you use them

[126]